BEYOND THE PAYCHECK

BEYOND THE PAYCHECK

Creating a Life of Wealth and Freedom

B. VINCENT

QuantumQuill Press

CONTENTS

CHAPTER 1

Introduction

This is about the spiritual aspects of finances and helping people build true wealth through planning, has a different outlook. Too often we see professionals who exceed their financial goals yet can't leave the office and the stress of their job, as well as working-class people who strain to get by no matter the current state of the economy. The human desire for freedom is based on the understanding that moments can be lived within the limits of autonomy, that those moments of freedom can provide excitement, or jolt one's life into something more interesting, more meaningful.

We need to think of money as a tool, a way to purchase and to invest in a life of joy, purpose, and freedom. For many who take refuge in clichés about magic money trees, freedom often boils down to having more money, reported that more than two-thirds of Americans are living paycheck to paycheck, which can have a serious impact on mental and financial well-being.

CHAPTER 2

Understanding Wealth and Freedom

If this plan for wealth and financial freedom is about reformulating the aims and attitudes behind dealing with money, doesn't that necessitate a discussion of wealth itself? These can be two distinct ideas. They usually are in most of society's discussions of each—it's just not the way we think about it. Having a clear picture of the destination makes the trek towards it more enjoyable and easier. So, with this chapter, I give a brief sketch of both wealth and freedom. I highlight what I think are crucial considerations (ideas typically lost in common discussions of money and general success) and discuss the relation between these. These ideas mentioned in this chapter are revisited later in the book in fuller discussions. Because wealth and freedom are important, great ideas, it's not too often they are given fuller treatments.

It matters that we learn to think about wealth as something beyond just the paycheck. I call the aim of financial independence "a life of wealth and freedom." This draws attention to the values and way of being that underlie pursuing FI, and also highlights that it is a life, rather than a goal, that we're barreling toward. It's possible to develop a strong Republican reflex at this. I hope you don't judge the merits of a life philosophy strictly based on the communities that often talk about it. Despite the disarray, the idea of flourishing and focusing on living a successful life remains appealing and important. Just take it from the ancient Greeks, a group that much of Western philosophy models ideas after.

CHAPTER 3

Assessing Your Current Financial Situation

The most important part of the complete process is figuring out your cash flow. You will need a statement to help you clarify this option. You can create your own or use a source of historical data. Try to go all the way back to the beginning of the year for the most accurate picture. You may have this type of information if you are participating in a budget monetary program like Quicken or Microsoft Money. You can also get the history of your financial system, which you may have either through income or expenses. Institutions that keep records include credit card institutions, banks, landlords (for those among you who make money from rental properties), and brokerages (in the case of stock accounts or any other types of needed accounts). It is your responsibility to create a veracious balance sheet at one point in your financial assessment. Fortunately, this need not be fifty pages long; a single page will do. It's a big assistance in measuring your slope.

It goes without saying that before you can move forward, you need to know where you're starting from. And, when it comes to money, most of us don't really know our starting point. That's because, like many people, you might have no idea how much you have coming in, how much is going out and where it's going. But, don't worry — you're going to be among the few who have taken the time to figure it all out. Congratulations! Here's what you're going to do on your financial assessment day. You're going to go through the following options, which will be a great learning experience. Don't worry. It may not be as horrendous as you believe. Let's get going.

CHAPTER 4

Setting Financial Goals

However, the big piece of the financial puzzle is investing effectively. Investing fundamentally entails using money and time to ensure that you have enough money even after you stop working due to old age or illness. Beginning at 20 years instead of age 30 might not make a huge difference in the present because it's the future results that really matter. Let's assume two investments earning 7% that have different lengths. Without doing any forecasting (which is difficult), the longer one would grow much bigger. If the savings accumulate for 40 years instead of 30 years, the saver would have close to 3x as much wealth. So start now, learn new ways to invest because that gives you more time for the interests to compound. Understand that the time frame selected for investment often affects the estimated future financial returns.

The challenge for most of us is not in knowing that we need to save. It is in knowing the best way to go about saving so that we have something to work with when the right opportunity comes along. In setting and achieving financial goals, we make better choices about things that matter to us. Some of the important financial goals that one needs to consider setting for themselves, or their family include:

building an emergency fund, creating daily and long-term budgets, paying off the student loan, and saving for retirement. Wealth can also be created by investing in popular assets such as physical properties, stocks, shares, and having a savings account. When setting financial bigger goals, always remember to follow the SMART criteria. Financial gurus explain that a goal to build an emergency fund of at least 6 months of your living expenses is a great first goal because it teaches you the discipline of saving for unpredictable events such as unemployment, home repairs, or significant medical bills.

CHAPTER 5

Developing a Wealth Mindset

Mindset is essential for everyone's well-being and living a life of wealth and freedom. Thoughts are constantly pouring out of our consciousness. What are you saying to yourself? The words you use to speak or put down onto paper (or laptop) guide your mental attitude or state, creating your reality. What message are you sending to yourself about your finances? Will fortune smile down upon you? Will the cash then appear when it is time to progress your thoughts and plans? How do you feel about wealth and are you striving to attract money? Your mental attitude toward wealth aims is essential as well. We require wealth to comprehend its importance in our lives and to establish that your financial status are as important as all other aspects of life. In essence, you are raising wealth to a level equal to your interpersonal relationships, life purpose, your drives and desires. This will reflect your intent to work with plenty and your individual requirements.

Having an invested and harmonious vision for our lives and wealth can typically make or break our financial future. You need information in order to grow and expand as a wealth builder. Having a wealth mindset and expanding your vision ensures your place at the peak of the wealth building continuum. At times life can be a whirlwind of emotions and in these instances it is key to make sure that we are connected to prosperity and our financial well-being. Unfulfilled desires can often cause our harmony to become muddy. When this is the case, it is clear we are not aligned with our highest potential. Understanding what prosperity and financial well-being mean to us as individuals is essential; this is also key in sustaining our wealth.

CHAPTER 6

Creating Multiple Streams of Income

Lack of time is often cited as the biggest hurdle. But the runaway success of remote working and contract work has resulted in more people with spare time. According to the General Social Survey, when looking at both free time and money, 75% of people who earn over $75,000 work just over 40 hours per week - not the superhuman careers that many believe. For Karem Suarez, a gourmet food professional, making time for her business venture was possible after she found an inherent passion for it. "It didn't feel as if I were working because I was engrossed in it," she says. Sharing your passion and expertise is likely how you're already spending your weekends and time off, so capturing that time can result in diverse income streams.

By now, having multiple income streams has become the standard. According to data from Charles Schwab, nearly half of people with a side gig say that it's boosted their income by as much as 20%. The most successful entrepreneurs have multiple forms of income, accounting for both unexpected market downturns and times of seasonal fluctuation. Side-gigs (or hobbies that could potentially become income sources) can include freelance writing, selling T-shirts on Shopify, or even professional dog-sitting.

CHAPTER 7

Investing for Long-Term Wealth

The basic, almost-uniform, investment strategy that most scholars, mutual fund managers, and investment counselors will tell you to embrace first is to invest in a diversified mix of assets. The goal is to boost your expected return as high as possible while also minimizing your risk (by selecting two investments that don't move in the same direction at the same time). This strategy's name is modern portfolio theory (MPT) but I will call it the "buy-hold-rebalance strategy" because that's what MPT looks like in real life.

In the last chapter, I presented a dozen possible investments where a beginning investor might start. Most of these ways to make your money grow weren't possible a few decades ago: very few people had credit cards or access to retirement plans or mutual funds or had even heard of annuities. You can feel grateful that we live in such an opportune time. You can open a brokerage account for the cost of a couple fancy drinks or use a charitable financial website that collects your spare change every day. Today, you have many great ways to make your money grow. Consider these alternatives and refine your investment strategy over time as you begin acquiring more capital and become more aware of the real you that I will reveal to you and then encourage you to follow.

CHAPTER 8

Building a Strong Financial Foundation

One of the repetitive themes Todd Strobel mentions is the fact that when it comes to building wealth, the most important factor is yourself. Yes, you have to think about the person in the mirror because you are the only one responsible for what you achieve. To put things in perspective, how many times have you distracted yourself by trying to imitate or copy someone else's success? It is a pitfall that everyone falls into at some point, and it is not a good place to be in. However, the reason that happens is because people usually don't have the right foundation. Without the right foundation, you will be running around in circles, jumping from one idea to another, and never really making any progress.

Welcome back to "Beyond the Paycheck". As always, we are excited to share gems of wisdom and advice. If you recall, in our previous sessions, we have been discussing the main ideas needed to build long-term wealth and freedom. We have discussed the importance of taking ownership and staying committed to a life of wealth and freedom. We have talked about how to develop better money habits, and the next course of action is focusing on building a strong financial foundation.

Managing Debt Effectively

Charge cards require full payment of the purchase price in a specified amount of time - usually on a monthly basis. They are usually acquired with the more prevalent companies earning a higher salary. If you make the payment within the specified time, you pay no interest. Ideally, this card is most appropriate for a person who is committed to executing major purchases within a limited time period. Unsecured credit cards have a prearranged spending limit. Interest rates can vary between 10% and 20%. By paying off when your bill is due, interest charges are avoided. People who have not had credit card payments for a longer time, such as college graduates, typically have to carry higher interest loans.

According to the New York Times article "Young Adult Shoppers Flag Credit Card Traps," the credit card issuer expects a college graduate to have an average of $9,000 of credit card debt by the time they have earned their degree. Unfortunately, the average is $3,200 more than the average credit card holder. To assist you with gaining positive credit management, consider the following. Prepaid credit cards require a person to deposit money prior to using the card. This way, a person could use the cash and your card without risking money you do not have. Be aware that some card charges often include charges for purchases and fees for monthly transfers and for closing of the prepaid account. Keep track of your major purchases by reviewing your bank account, credit card statement, and make a written record thereof. Keep the receipts related to these purchases in one folder. Squaring it with taxes at year-end is much easier this way.

Debt can be very expensive. It is the old bait and switch outlined. Not all debt is bad. Mortgages have tax benefits because the interest one pays on a mortgage is tax deductible. Mortgages are amortized - an interest rate that is often lower than other interest rates for longer-term loans. Tax advantages aside, paying for depreciating items using credit cards, payday loans, and/or fast cash advances too often typically ends in disaster. Think CRA for that. While a credit card may seem like a good choice for emergencies, it is not the best long-term solution. Have the attitude that you are working to live debt-free. Gaining control over accumulating debt should begin with not creating debt to begin with. Set long-term goals and short-term goals to help you stay on track toward eventual debt-free living. There is 1 year to those $400 dark sedans. Save and wait for it. High school and college graduates often receive credit card offers simply because they are new labor force members with earning potential. Because of this potential to earn, the card issuer believes the individual has possible repayment potential.

If you want to accumulate wealth, it is very important to understand the use of debt. Your wealth accumulation plan should not involve borrowing to acquire depreciating assets. Think about it, would it make sense to borrow to acquire a new car, LED television, or cashmere sweater? Not only do these items go down in value over time, they cost you extra to acquire when you add the high interest rate, despite the promise of 0% for the first 2 years.

CHAPTER 10

Maximizing Your Earning Potential

Understanding your market rate is also important. As a data analyst in 2018, the range for data analysts is $56,806 and $91,600. If four years down the line, I want to work in the public sector, I'd want to know that the public sector doesn't pay nearly as much.

Derek Magill has a new project called "How to Get Any Job You Want" that can walk you through the process of getting the job of your dreams. Salary negotiation is another key element of moving the ball when it comes to your compensation. How strong are your negotiation skills? When was the last time that you asked your boss for a raise? One negotiation tactic that I use at work is to help my coworkers understand the amount of money that I am losing out on when I'm at work because I'm not freelancing. And then I say that I won't freelance if my salary is doubled. Something to this effect.

A few years ago, I wrote a blog post about how to make a lot of money in the tech industry. The goal was to help people understand how they can earn a six-figure salary without needing multiple advanced degrees. Nearly 80% of jobs out there don't require anything more than a bachelor's degree. Those jobs are in the healthcare field, advanced manufacturing, and industrial production industries. It's a topic that I bang on quite a bit around here: the idea that you can make a lot of money early and often using your brain rather than your labor.

When it comes to finance, there's a lot of attention given to budgets, spending habits, and even scoring deals while shopping for everything from groceries to vacations. These are all important pieces of the puzzle. But while saving on expenses and shopping are important, there's one other element of having extra money in your life that is often overlooked: making more money.

CHAPTER 11

Building and Growing Your Business

For this matter, the other option, albeit typically time-consuming, is to learn as a team or finalize and maintain relationships with those who are experienced and who have gone before about building a business. The great news and terrible news is that there are continuous opportunities in today's environment, in every field, for those who are thinking through, searching for, thinking, and deciding on the correct product/service matching, the correct marketing and positioning mechanics, and targeting and closing the correct customer audience, on how to approach the management of building a company.

Another enormous challenge is managing the daily impact on your lifestyle and family life by the business's challenges, concerns, and demands for your ongoing personal analysis and proactive awareness. Clearly, this large, varied set of challenges and unknown factors can candidly encumber and even deter many of the most talented, technical business owners. Creating the right recipe for growing your idea into a financially-consistent, lifestyle business, and ultimately a more significant business, is a unique and difficult task for every business owner.

In reality, being in a business is extremely difficult, particularly in the beginning. Although the average business owner spends 60% of their time looking for clients with whom they may actually engage in research, provide services, and deliver the creative technology, in a start-up, even that number is significantly inflated. Scaling hours in the day and projecting revenues is tied to generating word of mouth, 'buzz,' and enough positive references, plus careful planning and follow-through for various other known success criteria, such as a relevant functional capability and market demand for your product or service, whether technology, support service, installation, or a combination of numerous needs.

Are you a landscaper who enjoys the freedom of the great outdoors but is also entrepreneurial and ambitious? Are you an automotive mechanic who prizes technical competence yet seeks to develop a network of those who share your passion for cars? Or are you a website designer who is intrigued with the process of creating clients' web pages but extremely skilled in delivering exemplary customer service while helping clients to look beyond the clutter of their day-to-day process and understand the potential of their website investment in their business? Regardless of your particular circumstances, the next logical step for some individuals is, in fact, to begin and grow a business within the industry (or profession) of their passion.

CHAPTER 12

Leveraging the Power of Networks

Today, when employees need to be hired, small business owners must analyze not only the professional competence of the specialist, but his alignment with the culture, values, and vision of the company. And the best way to see how capable and the person is what used to be its "abstract" attitudes, at that moment, external gestures, as it relates to others. Human relations heal successes and crises. That's powerful stuff. That is not totally new: in fact, it comes from the primal. But he fell out of favor with managers at large corporations and means of communication, tourism, and service in the developed world. Now, he comes back. Relationships are every day, the first step towards loyalty. More than money, personal relationships convey the integrity and the brand promise. Far beyond the paycheck, generational traits, except in the middle and upper classes, convey a lifestyle of social affluence and free time. Furthermore, it is a monetary issue. A person that a company retains has less loyalty to the competition and needs less incentive in the package.

We all know that relationships are important – in fact, they are perhaps the most rewarding aspect of our existence – and yet most seek a career "betterment of" approach using our intelligence and know-how to generate growth and professional success. This mind-set tends to separate personal life from career. But is it possible to achieve commercial success and a balanced lifestyle? If you are the creator of a business, is it possible to do it without sacrificing personal well-being?

CHAPTER 13

Embracing the Power of Passive Income

This important principle applies the logic of pyramid marketing but without its typical flaws, and by pairing it with the advantages of the Internet and its full power, we have been able to bring the multifaceted concept of leveraged income to a higher level. Emphasis is placed on the primary objective: complete independence achieved not only by personal action but also through optimal cooperation with others. This primary role is based on the strength of one's ability to attract an ever-increasing number of new clients and users of these services with a view to developing a flexible and gradually passive income. The leverage effect is further enhanced by the ability to encourage and support new business owners to perform in the same way. For the first time in the history of business, successful people are teaming up, their main priority as it turns out, being the creation of richness and financial independence of as many people as possible.

Leveraged income, the defining factor of passive or network income, is not new. In the context of the network economy, however, the concept of exploiting the leveraged force of the Internet along with the theory "the 80-20 rule" gives new meaning to it. The 80-20 rule announces that 80% of a company's income comes from 20% of the activity conducted by its salespeople. Thus, it is important for a company to make this cohort of its salespeople the richest possible in order to maximize income generation. The secret to achieving this is to allow each member of this sales team to create their earnings limit.

Here lies the secret to success in the information age – the creation of wealth and freedom through passive income. It is a well-known fact that the rich, the financially free, the successful create wealth and freedom through passive or, in other words, leveraged income. They get paid even while they are sleeping. Studies have shown that up to 90% of the income of successful people comes in a passive form. The significance of passive or leveraged income is well summarized in the statement made by Robert T. Kiyosaki, the celebrated author of the Rich Dad Poor Dad bestseller: "The rich don't work for money, they have people work for them."

CHAPTER 14

Protecting Your Wealth and Assets

Before you begin, the first thing you need to realize is the financial understanding that achieving financial success, most of the things people want to do and achieve it involves having a strong financial position to maintain a life of wealth. Rights are where legislation mandates or guarantees that an industry or country will provide citizens with a certain set of protection. Things here in the US would be Social Security, retirement accounts, pensions, Medicare, and health insurance. The earth we live on is a single entity that is made up of natural resources. Resources that can be gone if we are not careful around her. She is affected by actions made by man on a daily basis. This section of the Treasury would now include Global Warming, Greenhouse Gases, climate reforms, and Renewable Energy. The Federal Government listed protecting citizens as one of the primary reasons we formed our Republic and Constitution. We were unable to protect ourselves alone and must have this collective group to protect ourselves better. Section four of the First Article lists the Obligations of the States.

Most people think of wealth as money and assets, and of building a life of wealth as building financial success. Building a life of wealth is, in many ways, protecting the success you will have. Financial success is only a part of the process of living a life of wealth. Billy Graham said, "A real and lasting wealth only means one thing - and that's life... for riches and wealth are of no lasting value when we are dead." This is not an infomercial world of "as seen on TV" get rich quick schemes. It is a world of ethical behavior and moral values. It is about valuing yourself and what you have to offer and how you approach others in any given endeavor.

Estate Planning and Wealth Transfer

The smaller your estate, the more you need an estate plan. In a way, the very wealthy have it easy. Estate tax laws allow them to transfer large amounts to their heirs free of any federal estate tax. But for those of you with smaller estates, there are essential tools to help you distribute not only your financial assets, but also your retirement accounts and life insurance in the most beneficial and controlled manner possible. To go beyond the paycheck and create a life of wealth and freedom you have to protect your cash flow in addition to creating your net worth. Individuals of all monetary levels need an estate plan that includes more than just a will or living trust. You can use processes that allow the assets in your retirement account to go where you want them to go, bypassing probate, capitalizing the required distribution after your death, extend the benefits of the retirement account to younger generations in your family, and provide your beneficiaries with an asset protection shield.

When you hear the term "estate planning," you may think only of taxes, wills, and other legal documents. While these are part of the puzzle, estate planning encompasses much more. Your estate includes all of your assets that you own while you are alive and does not just mean the will or living trust that distributes your assets when you pass away. Estate planning involves planning, in advance, so that everything you worked for can go where you want it to go in the most tax efficient and hassle-free manner possible. And, wills and living trusts are just two of many tools used to accomplish this. Just like a corporation uses several tools to operate, such as accounting software, a telephone system, and procedures, and does not depend on just one thing, estate planning is a process that uses several tools that are integrated smoothly to accomplish a set of goals.

CHAPTER 16

Balancing Wealth and Personal Well-being

3.7 Wealth and Personal Well-being So far, we have only considered the instrumental function of privilege to compound advantages, with little attention to how privileged people actually feel. Yet, the most common finding from happiness research is that money is necessary for happiness, but it does not guarantee happiness beyond a basic level of survival. However, these studies usually only look at people from privileged nations. What happens if you are already a part of the privileged 1%? Why do we keep working so hard? What do we do with the wealth once we have it? Some studies have confirmed mere materialism is not associated with well-being. In particular, money buys happiness only when it is experientially spent on others, on the self, on leisure, and on less arduous work. Simply put, money may be happiness in rich nations to make us equal based on high costs of living and bills to pay, but—when presented with the choice of how we spend it—money may be happiness only when we spend it in ways that maintain social status yet sharply depart from mere materialism alone.

If high-flyers are frequently both politically connected and wealthy in ideal cosmetics, thus the ideal cosmetics of high privilege went beyond cosmetics to include wealth. This result suggests white elites use their advantages to truly have it all. However, it may also seem counterintuitive with racial rhetoric suggesting whites need to work hard in order to succeed. Perhaps these findings result from differences in racialization processes for low-status versus high-status groups—for example, the idea of Asians being inherently competitive compared to the stereotype of lazy Blacks.

CHAPTER 17

Living a Life of Purpose and Fulfillment

Do you think that God created us with the same purpose? Our purpose can't just be to work all our lives just to then retire. Do we really just come here to be served, go through painful hardships to not even learn from them, to never leave significant change in the world? When we leave this world, the only thing we take is the experience we have, the people we've become along the years, and what we left behind for others. Everything you do, everything you bring into this world will remain long after you're gone. It's true, at least, that it has the potential to endure. This is what people today lack a lot, a sense of purpose, and not just one. We are beings with an infinite ability to create. If we are where we are with our intellect, it's because we were created with this vastness of ideas!

"What's your why?" Today, in this economy, you have to have a strong passion for what you do. So, what's your "big why?" It can't just be money or shallow things. You can't be doing it just because you want to show off. You can't be obsessed by your spouse because even that has dangerous consequences. For the thing that once drove you to get up very early doesn't last, it fades, and without a solid, balanced "why," things fall apart. We are not just here to work every day to pay off debts and bills. We can't be here just to live for paychecks!

CHAPTER 18

Giving Back and Making a Difference

If his book persuades you that Kirk's journey is within reach for you as well, he hopes you use the substantial freedom and wealth you create for the good of all humanity. Making yummy jam can increase the world's happiness (and even its GDP). So far, no one has gone broke helping others! Sharon donates her incredible time and energy to many great causes. She annually volunteers 500 or more hours teaching younger students at her former college, she has served on three mayoral appointed task forces, and she's held numerous leadership roles in many non-profits. When she was named Business Woman of the Year by the Women's Council in her city, she turned the honor into a thank-you/fund-raiser for the local humane society. In short, Kirk and Sharon believe in the power of each and every human to make a positive difference. Sharon has proven that one's impact depends less on how frequently you attempt to make a difference and more on the determination and consistency with which you apply the power of the human spirit to fuel your quest to spark change.

Kirk is a strong supporter of not-for-profit organizations. He and Sharon believe in the power of each individual creating a positive difference. Time has been Kirk's most visible and valuable contribution, but donations and occasional direct project assistance from both Kirk and Sharon have made a small difference in several organizations. Only time will tell whether the many seeds they've helped plant will continue to grow. Kirk has long hoped to be able to make a more substantial and sustained difference, and that hope is part of what's driven him to craft the life of wealth and freedom he describes in the book's final chapter.

Overcoming Financial Obstacles and Challenges

You have to prepare for the unforeseen financial roadblocks because they'll come. I had a friend in my early twenties who used to tell me, "Grant, it's not how you fall down that matters, it's how you get up." Understand this too. These eventualities are simply life lessons from your Wealth Account. Acknowledge the mistakes or circumstances, and move forward. Athletes and achievers fail time and time again. The person who keeps going and never relents is the person who succeeds at the highest level. Oprah Winfrey's story is a classic example. She was told she was unfit for television but she persevered. Michael Jordan was kicked off his high school basketball team, and Michael W. Young wanted to be a professional hockey player but failed. His Plan B was becoming a multi-millionaire with Scentsy. Walt Windham, the founder of the M1 "fitness phenomenon," appeared on a show called Gulfcoast Wrestling on Spike TV, and not only was he the last man in a Royal Rumble, but he also manhandled professional wrestler/actor Hulk Hogan. Walt ultimately utilized the skills and lessons he learned in the financial world and shared them with celebrities and grateful fans.

Paycheck to create a Wealth Account. Everyone has roadblocks, hurdles, and naysayers in life. Whether it's a financial lapse, a real estate closing gone wrong, a career setback, or a personal life tragedy, the truth is, stuff happens! You may experience financial hiccups like a job loss, a divorce, a decrease in salary, or a health issue that creates a drain on your Wealth Account. It's going to happen at some time, so be ready. How you deal with life's challenges will determine your outcome. You can let a financial setback debilitate you, or you can allow it to empower you. I hope you will choose the latter.

CHAPTER 20

Navigating Economic Changes and Uncertainty

There are two things you can count on in an economy: uncertainty and change. It's a predictable fact that prices for goods and services will go up. This is known as inflation. Additionally, you can depend on the fact that taxes are sure to increase. In the business world, employers need to stay abreast on strategies that prevent price erosion and strategies to protect profits. It is critical that most Americans develop a 'full employment' strategy to increase their earning potential or at the very least to keep up with the rising costs of goods and services in an economy. A different approach to compensation is required. As the economists forecast, the future is about the contingency to self-agents. This market uses agility as motor instead of the duration property that is traditionally perceived as the best solution for the payment of short-term or long-term work.

One thing you can count on in an economy is uncertainty and change. We know for sure prices of goods and services will go up. Inflation will continue. Taxes will go up too. Business owners will have to keep their prices in alignment with costs and generate strategies to protect profits. Most Americans will have to figure out 'full employment' strategies for themselves if they wish to keep up or maintain purchasing power for themselves.

CHAPTER 21

Embracing a Growth Mindset

Some of our experiences in this life have the power to inform, modify, and condition all of our future experiences, living our calling, and the reality that we create. Properly managing these experiences and using them as learning tools or opportunities for inner knowledge and understanding is essential. A lot of people let these experiences define who they are, and worst, dictate where their future is headed. We all need to embrace the knowledge and understanding that experiences bring and understand that they, in addition to conditioning, finding strength and understanding the reasons and lessons around them, also teach a lot about the capacity of our inner growth and resourcefulness. We all know that forced growth can be very - or extremely - painful, and it usually is. However, if we embrace the love of life and choose to see the lessons at hand and allow it to touch our hearts and nourish our souls, then growth becomes a growth track without stumbling, and the pain tends to be non-existent or very short-lived, if the pain is present at all.

Growing up as a fresh immigrant from Africa had a deep impression on me, especially with money and abundance. During my transition and integration in Canada, I did not think about abundance. It was quite the opposite; my parents, big sister, little brother, and I lined up at the Food Bank regularly. I only thought about what others had that I did not and could not afford. Our reality shaped a fixed mentality in me, and my growth process was slow and painful, although rewarding in the end. The reality of our living and survival conditions (this was before I turned 19) had a profound impact on me and my relationship with money. I thought that the goodness of my heart, and my painful life experiences, would lead to a rewarding life and financial wealth in the end. After all, that's what I had seen in most of the Hollywood movies that I loved to watch.

CHAPTER 22

Cultivating Positive Habits for Financial Success

Estimate how much is enough and live with margin. Decide what is enough money. Explain what you would do if only given eighteen months, how you would invest and for how long. When you receive enough money at the start, when you have more than a decade to establish wealth, this will likely be what you want to achieve. Furthermore, the more money you have at your disposal, the easier it becomes for you to spend. Also, people with a goal are three times more likely to achieve their goal than are those without a plan. Be goal-oriented and develop ongoing daily habits. You'll edge out the less educated, less fortunate, and less self-disciplined to create your best life ever, yet you won't aim too high or too low.

When it comes to financial success, most self-made millionaires agree that the habits you cultivate on a daily basis will determine your financial success, ultimately lowering your stress. Consider these habits, knowing that the most successful of these factors are practiced by more than 90 percent of multimillionaires. Live within your means. Only one in three of these highly successful individuals would advocate for spending less than you make as the best path to wealth, but roughly 80 percent of self-made millionaires champion this strategy. Get your priorities in order and establish your value system so that you create a plan for living beneath your means.

Mastering the Art of Negotiation and Persuasion

A confident investor is able to paint a clear picture in the minds of potential investors, strategic partners, or those they want to recruit. They're able to put themselves in their shoes and convince them how they can help solve specific problems facing the other side. They leverage any and all positive stereotypes that people have when dealing with someone of their kind and break down the negative ones. At the same time, they're comfortable scrutinizing the specific requirements they'll need when seeking financing or a specific type of partnership. Remember, wealth is an outside reflection of the problem you solved. We all have a car and we all have 5 friends and we all have a Facebook account, not because it's bad, but because they are solving a specific problem and we are willing to pay and repeatedly pay for that problem to be solved.

A master negotiator isn't someone who's able to dominate and berate the other side. Rather, that person is able to persuade. They're able to paint a clear and vivid picture in the minds of the other side, at the same time breaking down and attacking the negative stereo-types that people have when dealing with someone of their kind. Persuasion, not fighting, is the key to winning the big arguments. Persuasion is what creates allies, and persuasion is what changes the world. It was the key to winning the big arguments in my career. It can be at the heart of everything you do, every day.

CHAPTER 24

Developing Financial Intelligence and Literacy

Financial illiteracy is one of three primary ways people become rich, middle class, or poor. Every time you go to work, the government takes money out of your paycheck in the form of taxes. There are three kinds of earnings workers can make: earned income, passive income, and portfolio income. The major problem is that there are people who have jobs and make a good income, but because they have not learned how to handle money, they allow financial institutions to take it. Everyone needs to master money in order to enjoy all the good things like the company of good friends, the thrill of sports, appreciation of art, the healthcare to cure infections, the faith in God who is worthy of trust. If we know how to handle our money we can obtain these things and be happy forever after. The good news is that though painful and difficult, it is not at all a difficult skill to develop if we have the willpower or courage to be disciplined.

Having financial intelligence involves understanding numbers and being able to work well with math and patterns. People who have musical intelligence use notes and sounds to think, and those with high in numbers like me need patterns and numbers to think. Understanding the way money works in people's lives. Financial intelligence can be seen as a modeling strategy of the individual values, complexities, interconnections and interactions, and temporal memory. People who use numbers as their thinking strategies are more likely to use numbers in their everyday life to make a living and rely less on those who do not use numbers. A rational argument insists that if you are good at the game, you are more likely to play well, while not being able to play well at present may lead you to not play at all in the future. However, the ignorance on testing in future research of the direction of the association between mathematical ability and financial literacy still requires testing before any firm conclusions or policy implications can be derived from the present study.

CHAPTER 25

Harnessing the Power of Technology for Financial Success

One often hears that "Knowledge Is Power." This is the message echoed by well-meaning financial advisors, mentors, and teachers. The power is ultimately technology based. The computer, Internet, and networking intuitively provide the tools and support network that gives the user the entrée to a "secret society." How to use the power of technology to enhance education is the focus of this research study. The typical approach is through the development and use of a financial decision-making tool accessible to the common individual. The tool proposed is designed to enhance the learning experience, inspire the use visual and statistical representation of data resulting from a variety of parameter choices, remind users of sound financial principles, and provide consequence-based reinforcement and financial rewards.

Some of the failures in attaining financial security are thought to be the results of lack of understanding, lack of discipline and reinforcement, and lack of trust in the process. Regardless of one's level of experience, it is helpful to have access to instructional, analytical, and operational hands-on software to bridge the gap between wistful hope and realistic expectation. Armed with strong product, technical data, and industry knowledge, the user is more likely to overcome those dangerous self-imposed roadblocks. It is our intention here to help facilitate the process associated with attaining financial security by using new and emerging technologies in the area of software tools on the user (open) and provider (closed) side to give a measure of educational enhancement, entertainment, and profitably exploitable information.

CHAPTER 26

Exploring Alternative Investment Opportunities

Investment alternatives are relevant to this discussion in that they provide one of three proven strategies for recreating successful investor returns. In short, successful investors produce superior returns by including unique investment-exploiting strategies that are not available to poor investors. For instance, cash is the only asset that can be loaned without turnover or volume constraints - and lending cash is exactly how successful investors earn returns as the counterpart of margin loans. While they might also be shorting securities at the same time, the activity of shorting is not important in terms of the return generated on the cash, unless there are downward micro-structure liquidity surprises in the borrowing market for shares and fixed-income exchange-traded funds.

For the past three decades, the investment industry has advanced opportunities beyond the traditional stock and bond products. From 1980-2000, precious metals, natural resources, real estate, and international equities produced superior returns to the overall equity return of the S&P 500, and the number of alternative investment choices for financial planners and successful investors has grown linearly. These investment alternatives might be categorized as asset-specific investment segments, fixed-income type investments, and private placements. Among the advantages of these investments are lower market-quality pricing through price discovery, lower correlation of returns to the traditional investments, and less market fragmentation with arbitrage constraints. Among the three investment categories, private placements offer the most unique opportunities. As such, this overview covers detailed discussions of not only Hedge Funds and other four private placements, but also of venture capital and private real estate.

CHAPTER 27

Achieving Financial Independence and Early Retirement

To be clear, financial independence isn't an all-or-nothing activity. In essence, achieving financial independence occurs when your life experiences and retrospective provoke the realization that money is not an object. Once your assets and future earning potential are sufficient to provide for your lifestyle with the utmost enjoyment and comfort for the rest of your life, you have reached financial independence. In this way, achieving financial independence simply necessitates that your resources will exceed your expenses for the rest of your life. This goal allows for certain individuals to retire with confidence (depending on how achievable their doomsday predictions are), while others will be prompted to continue pursuing the things that make them happy. I, for one, believe that finding a meaningful time-filling activity will be essential to avoid an early death post-retirement.

Retiring early and frequently traveling the world isn't for everyone, but with an increasingly popular movement called the Financial

Independence (FI) community, many young and old individuals are speeding up their life's clock towards an early retirement. While escaping the traditional path of aging, working, and acquiring more unused toys is difficult, the achievement of financial independence isn't out of reach. All it takes to accomplish this feat is creating a plan during your working career and sticking to your defined objectives during both well-planned and the more unexpected situations. Once you pass the point in life where you achieve financial independence, the choice to continue working, not making money, or ditching the safety nets in your current professional career will be entirely up to you.

CHAPTER 28

Traveling and Experiencing the World

One of the most popular experiences in life is traveling and experiencing the world. The sights, sounds, tastes, and customs of populations residing in different parts of the world give insight into things previously unknown or misunderstood. The majority of people desire to travel. However, there are plenty who inadvertently make traveling sound boring. A boring trip is valued more often by a person for the mere increased enjoyment of their routine comforts rather than unique experiences and learning opportunities. A person who is described as multicultural knows and understands multiple cultures and comports themselves with a higher level of class and emotional intelligence, as they are better adept at learning and adopting adaptive insights of various cultural styles.

To uncover the various types of work that each of us may engage in, listen to yourself, then do what feels right to you and try new things. The "going along with the plan" attitude will likely leave you unfulfilled and with pent-up resentment after a while. This is because the majority of people in this world do not know how to consider the type of work that has meaning to them and understand that wealth and money from pursuing a hobby or original passion, workplace happiness, and freedom are achievable, rather than impossible abstracts. A person whose individual type of work and individual type of wealth are the same – who does work that is how they enjoy being alive and is their reason for being alive – will always have wealth and satisfaction. Plenty of financially successful people have said just as much: "I am the happiest by doing those things that others might find demanding, restricted, or non-remunerative."

CHAPTER 29

Building Strong Relationships and Networks

Be very selective about who you spend time with. Be wary of relationships that are unbalanced and stressful, and instead focus your energy on nurturing friendships with low-maintenance, supportive friends. The best friendships are straightforward, honest, and unselfish. A good friend is someone who can provide sound advice, help guide you in the right direction, and truly support and care about you, your best interests, and your personal growth. For a friendship to be healthy, it's essential that both people exhibit self-love and respect. Avoid people who are negative, pushy, undependable, and those who are constantly overwhelmed with their own lives. These people will not only fill your life with unnecessary chaos, they'll pull you away from your vision of a trouble-free, simple, free life. This includes family. If a family member causes you unwarranted drama, pain, and stress by way of their hidden agendas, disrespect, or other means, you are well within your right to avoid this toxicity.

Make sure you spend time developing and nurturing solid, positive relationships with a variety of people in your life. Everyone can enrich your life in some way, even if they don't have the resources you do. Some are wise and can give you excellent advice from their own life experiences, while others have the potential of adding extraordinary value to your sporting or hobby community. Others may just lend an empathetic ear and offer kind words of understanding when you need it most. Valuable relationships are just as much about you giving as others contributing to you. Give back to your community. Join service organizations, participate in community events, or contribute to a charity. Giving back will not only allow you to feel good about yourself, it's a great way to grow your social network and raise your visibility in the community. People generally like people who do good in the world and are likely to remember and support you when you need help.

CHAPTER 30

Finding Balance Between Work and Life

In just seven fast steps, you'll be able to participate in activities such as completing surveys, joining in classroom or group discussions, or chatting with friends. This particular step allows for an open mind, helping others to better make sense of their surroundings. But before we begin, you must follow these three easy directions: Please take the time to participate in the activities provided for each section. By doing this, you will be given an opportunity for group involvement and the chance to experience a viewpoint unlike anything you'll hear from me. Sharing in the process of thinking, you'll find gender-based interruptions that interrupt analytical thought diminishing while also embracing the understanding that you may or may not be alone in experiencing unique thoughts such as these.

Work. We all have to do it, right? But have you ever shared your mantra for work with a close friend, only to earn a quizzical look? Do any of these complaints sound familiar? "I'm so sick of working these long hours. Who has time with family anymore?" or "I'm married to my job and I don't even get a paycheck!" It doesn't just come in long hours, either. No matter your understanding of a "good," life-giving job, there is a need for balance. For generations prior to the Baby Boomers, long hours, small pay, and days interrupted by work meant only that, but today, there is a greater push toward work-life integration. YES! You do have homework! Designed to aid in reflection and critical thinking, the Exercise/Reach Out section requires you to consider the concepts outlined in the chapters, such as Career Skills, Pride, and Social and Personal Values.

CHAPTER 31

Continuing Education and Lifelong Learning

Never stop learning. Continuing education is particularly important for leaders because the expectations of a high-ranking business executive or thought leader in any field are high. When you are in a position of power or leadership, people are naturally expecting you to think smarter than the average Joe, advise them well, and be at the top of your game. Regularly refreshing your knowledge base on one hand keeps your mental faculties performing at their best, and on the other helps with the requirements of the job. During the course of your continuing education, it is up to you to specify how much time you will dedicate to both formal and self-learning. Formally learning in an educational institution and learning from the field experiences you have honed your practical skills. Both types of learning are critical for personal development. Unfortunately, many of us learn less over time because (1) we become less open to new knowledge as we get older and (2) many organizations do not consistently support employee learning.

In the rapidly changing technological world, the life span of any knowledge base is continually shrinking. It's said that the half-life of an engineer's knowledge is about 18 months, which translates to having half a working knowledge of material less than two years old. As Dr. Isaac Asimov once said, "The only constant is change, continuing change, inevitable change, that is the dominant factor in society today." As an engineer, I know too well from my education at MIT that it is necessary to continually upgrade one's learning. Still, personal experience has taught me that as necessary as continuing education is for an engineer, it is equally critical for business executives and leaders. Pursuit of a lifetime of knowledge should not end when you have an MBA or are promoted to a significant leadership role. That's what I tell my kids.

CHAPTER 32

Conclusion

Building a life of wealth and freedom requires taking prudent risks in both your professional and personal lives and never allowing money or power to dictate what you love. To do this, you need to find an environment that can support people who take risks, and who calculate those risks well. Risk assumption seems ingrained in my desire for freedom. I have reasoned my way through various preferences and the business decisions that I make because a key driver of my happiness is achieving freedom. This explains why my happiness often escalates with increased responsibilities and is independent of increased burdens. I liken this to the feelings of responsibility that parents feel for their children: parasitic in nature. This is the secret to the abundance in my life.

I learned very early in life that money was not the only important form of compensation. Doing work that I found compelling and that gave me the freedom and flexibility to be available for my family was much more important than the paycheck I would earn. When I allowed the working environment I found myself in to get in the way of something that was more important than money, I ultimately lost the money because I could not sustain the environment. Being resilient allows you to thrive on change and take the initiative to create change, to remain entrepreneurial, and to love the opportunities that come your way. To avoid feeling risk and scaling boundaries to foster their own growth.